Original title:
Ripples of the Lost Tides

Copyright © 2025 Creative Arts Management OÜ
All rights reserved.

Author: Kieran Blackwood
ISBN HARDBACK: 978-1-80587-450-8
ISBN PAPERBACK: 978-1-80587-920-6

Reflections of a Distant Past

Once a fish wore a fancy hat,
He danced with crabs and sang to cats.
Time flew by, he lost his groove,
Now he just floats, his moves to prove.

A jellyfish ate his stylish threads,
With tentacles flailing, it danced with dreads.
The ocean laughed, waves rolled with glee,
While our hat-wearing fish just wanted tea.

The Weight of Time Beneath the Surface

An old whale tells tales of yore,
Of pirate ships and treasure galore.
But instead of gold, they found some socks,
Now he brags 'bout those stinky rocks.

Dolphins play tricks, a prank and a splash,
Turning the tide with a huge, silly clash.
Time may weigh heavy beneath the waves,
But laughter's the treasure that every heart craves.

Solitary Songs of the Misty Isles

A lonely seagull sings to the wind,
With a tune that makes dolphins grin.
Misty isles are where he roams,
But his jokes are corny, like old sea foam.

He mimics the waves with a comical flap,
While crabs roll their eyes and nap in a lap.
The sun chuckles down, lighting up the show,
As the seagull sings songs that no one will know.

Where the Sea Meets Its Echo

At dusk when the sea whispers low,
An echo replies, 'You go, I go!'
They play tag 'round rocks, such merry old chums,
While barnacles laugh, drumming their drums.

'You're too shallow!' the echo will tease,
'But I'm deep in thoughts—oh, please don't freeze!'
They swap silly tales of fish with long beards,
Creating a chorus that nobody hears.

Murmurs of the Underlying Deep

In the ocean's playful grin,
Seaweed dances, full of sin.
Crabs in tuxedos, on parade,
While fish gossip, quite dismayed.

Starfish flipping through the flow,
Playing tag with algae glow.
Mermaids giggle, lose their scale,
As dolphins sneak a fruity fail.

Vanished Hopes on Tidal Shores

A sock was lost, dear ocean wide,
It waves goodbye, with grumpy tide.
Seagulls cackle, dive for fun,
While beach balls dance under sun.

Footprints sprint, then wash away,
Sandcastle dreams beginning to sway.
Wild crabs boast about their loot,
As flip-flops scamper, just a hoot!

The Dance of Time-Worn Waters

Old boats sway with style and grace,
Sailors wink, a fun-filled race.
Jellyfish jiggle, what a sight,
Lighting up the waves at night.

Whales make jokes and tell tall tales,
Splashing water with their trails.
Octopuses throw a wild bash,
With party hats, they make a splash!

Cries of the Abandoned Coast

A lighthouse flickers, gives a laugh,
Rocks grumble, grumpy little staff.
Seashells whisper secrets they keep,
While beach bums snooze, all in a heap.

Tides trip over, have a blast,
Candles flicker, shadows cast.
Old buoys chat about their fame,
Though no one knows their sacred name.

Murmurs from the Deep

Underwater gags make fish all giggle,
Scuba gear dances, it does a little wiggle.
A clam jokes, 'I'm sure I'm not that shellfish!'
While eels argue over who's the best myth!

Bubbles rise up, carrying tales so silly,
The octopus clowning, oh what a willy-nilly!
With seaweed wigs and starfish for a fool,
They laugh like crazy, in this watery school!

Fading Currents of Memory

Old boats creak tales of salt and laughter,
Their wood is weathered, hear stories after.
Fish tales grow taller, like waves at high tide,
Where all the big ones seem to try and hide.

Remembrances drift in a humorous spin,
Did I catch a tuna, or was it a tin?
As surfboards float by, funny clouds roll on,
In past splashes of joy, our memories are drawn!

Ghosts of the Distant Shore

Ghost crabs are dancing, their moves are absurd,
Grabbing with pincers, oh wasn't that heard?
With a jig and a shuffle, they cross upon sand,
Making shy sea turtles clap their flippers in hand.

Echoes of laughter on the wind softly moan,
As sea gulls throw jokes, each winged one's a clown.
A phantom fish swims with an unshakeable grin,
While memories of fun leave no room for sin!

Traces of What Once Was

Footprints dance lightly, then wash away fast,
Leaving only whispers, remnants of past.
Where did my bucket go? Did it swim away?
Did the tide take my shovel? Oh what a day!

A shovel and pail scheming by the tide,
Dreaming of castles where snails can reside.
With laughter that echoes like bubbles in air,
The traces we leave are even more rare!

Whispers of Distant Shores

Sandy toes and jellyfish jokes,
Seagulls chat like silly folks,
Sunscreen spills, a slippery feat,
Dancing crabs in rhythmic beat.

Splashing waves with playful glee,
Fish in shades of pink and brie,
A boat that drifts with pizza scent,
And mermaids on their time well spent.

Echoes Beneath the Surface

In the depths where fishes sing,
Octopi wear hats in spring,
A turtle whispers tales so grand,
Of treasure maps drawn in the sand.

Bubbles rise with giggles loud,
Clams get shy, beneath their shroud,
The seaweed sways, with laughter bright,
As dolphins jump, oh what a sight!

Secrets of the Moonlit Current

Underneath the silver beams,
Starfish share their wildest dreams,
Crabs crave snacks from land above,
While snails send notes of seaweed love.

The moon winks down, in a playful jest,
Sea cucumbers in their Sunday best,
Nudibranchs flaunt colors galore,
As jellyfish boogie on the ocean floor.

Shadows on the Water's Edge

At twilight's call, the fish don masks,
In the tide pools, mischief basks,
Starry skies cast curious glows,
While frogs in tuxedos strike a pose.

Crickets chirp their jazz-filled tunes,
The sun dips low, kissing balloons,
With every splash, a giggle soars,
As shadows play on salty shores.

The Unraveling of Submerged Stories

In the depths where stories swim,
Fish tell tales on a whim.
Seagulls giggle, waves a-dance,
Each shell hiding a secret chance.

Octopuses spin yarns quite bold,
While crabs find their treasure, untold.
A mermaid's laugh, a chuckle bright,
Making waves from morning to night.

Forgotten Portals of the Ocean's Hold

A door with seaweed hanging loose,
What lies behind? Perhaps a moose!
Jellyfish flutter, with socks askew,
Wondering if they need a shoe.

Starfish ponder their cosmic fate,
Did someone order a cosmic plate?
With forks for fish, and spoons for brine,
Dinner served at half past nine.

The Eternal Song of Abandoned Harbors

Sails that flap like laundry lines,
Creaking ships share silly signs.
Barnacles complain with whispering tones,
As sea turtles nod in hushed moans.

Whales compose a wobbly tune,
Echoing off the pale, round moon.
As gulls join in with squawky glee,
It's a party for all under the sea.

Cascading Memories in Salty Air

A bottle's salute from days gone by,
Held a note from a clam with a sigh.
Shimmering sands offer up a jest,
With sunbathers joining the ocean's quest.

Tides toss laughter in each wave,
Crabs tap dance, delightfully brave.
As seagulls find a snack or two,
Who knew the sea could be this fun too?

The Silence of Forgotten Waves

Waves that crash with a thud so loud,
Yet silence reigns where fish once bowed.
Seagulls squawk, they've lost their groove,
Dancing jellies, who needs to move?

Starfish hiding, they've missed the show,
While crabs join in, with their best toe-to-toe.
Sandcastles crumbled, they gave up the fight,
As the tide rolled in, laughing with delight.

Traces in the Sand

Footprints drawn in a doodle of fun,
Mysteries linger of who could run.
Was it a toddler, or maybe a cat?
Or perhaps a mermaid in the shape of a hat?

Each wave that licks at the shore so sly,
Wipes away stories, oh me, oh my!
Yet sand's still sticky, like a jelly's kiss,
In this sandy dance, who could resist?

Reflections of What Once Was

Mirrors in water where laughter refracts,
Fishing for giggles, the sea simply acts.
An octopus grins, wearing a hat,
While clams clap shells, now imagine that!

Seaweed sways like a curious dancer,
As crabs take a stroll with style and swagger.
What was once serious now feels so bright,
Under moonlit giggles of soft shining light.

Faded Footprints in Seafoam

Footprints washed out, they chuckle with ease,
At secrets they're keeping, like whispers in the breeze.
A dolphin chuckles, it's all in good fun,
While sea cucumbers bask in the sun.

Each bubble bursts with tales to unfold,
Of crabs and their parties, so daring, so bold.
As foam frolics on shores like a playful dog,
Life's a funny mess, like a comical fog!

Specters Beneath the Calm

Beneath the waves, they dance around,
With flippers flapping, no solid ground.
A ghostly fish, in a hat so bright,
Swims in circles, all through the night.

Jellybeans float, with whispers so loud,
Caught in a net, a mischievous crowd.
They play hide and seek, but oh what a tease,
Bobbing like corks, with giggles and wheezes.

A squid in a tux, at the underwater ball,
Tried to waltz, but stumbled and fell.
Crabs clap their claws, in raucous delight,
As the clownfish swims, in a frantic flight.

"Is that a seaweed salad?" one merman cried,
As a sea cucumber slid down the tide.
With laughter and merriment, the ocean's best,
They render the quiet, a hilarious jest.

Phantoms in the Ocean's Embrace

In swirling currents where shadows play,
Phantoms frolic at the end of the day.
A seal wearing shades, sunbathing with flair,
Fins up in the air, without a care.

A flatfish pranks with a sneaky glide,
Making kids giggle—best ride ever tried.
They flip and flop, from side to side,
Sliding on sea glass like an ocean slide.

"Oh please don't stare!" the ghost crab said,
"I'm more than my shell," so proudly he led.
With a wink and a scuttle, he dashed away,
Leaving behind laughter in the salty spray.

A treasure chest grins, with coins made of brass,
While octopuses juggle, they're quite the class!
Show boater fish flip, in sequined delight,
The phantoms in tow, vanish into the night.

A Lament for the Unseen Waves

Once there were waves that laughed and sang,
But now they whisper, a phantom's clang.
A sea horse yawns, with a sleepy pout,
As the tides drift slowly and slip out.

"Why so solemn?" a mermaid exclaimed,
"Just because the tide seems a little ashamed?"
A whale with a wink, replied with a cheer,
"I've got the best jokes, come lend me your ear!"

Caught off guard by a droll octopus,
Who spills spaghetti, in clean ocean's fuss.
"Dinner's gone wild," he chuckled with glee,
As seagulls circled, "That's quite the spree!"

But through the water, a silly swirl,
Reminds us all, of the fun in this world.
So raise your shells, let the laughter flow,
For unseen waves still dance, don't you know?

Sighs of the Abyss

In the depths, a fish wore a tie,
He danced and flopped, oh my, oh my!
A whale blew bubbles that formed a grin,
While jellyfish giggled, let the fun begin.

A crab tried to breakdance, slipped on a shell,
His pals cheered loudly, 'Hey, that's swell!'
With snickers and splashes, the sea joined in,
Such nonsense brought laughter, a bubbly din.

A starfish joked, 'I'm missing a foot!'
'But I've got five!' the clownfish hoot.
They traded bad puns like treasures obscure,
In this underwater land, laughter's the cure.

The Solitude of Salty Breezes

A parrot squawks while perched on a dock,
'Why did the crab wear a blue polka dot?'
He roasts the poor crustacean all day,
While seagulls form a choir, attempting to sway.

The shores are alive with a hammock of jokes,
The tides chime in, 'We're the real folks!'
An octopus juggles with flair and finesse,
'Who knew we had talent? We're truly a mess!'

As waves rolled in, they carried a laugh,
A fish in a bowtie said, 'I need a staff!'
With fins flapping freely, the fun would restart,
In breezy solitude, they all played their part.

A Tapestry of Drowned Stories

In waters where tales get tangled and spun,
A mermaid exclaimed, 'I'm the queen of fun!'
She told of the sailor who lost his boot,
While a dolphin burst forth with a cartwheel salute.

They gathered the seaweed for laughter and cheer,
A treasure map leading to giggles, oh dear!
'Follow the bubbles to Pinocchio's tale,'
Whispered an octopus, who'd set out to sail.

With sea turtles laughing at their own pace,
They shared seaweed snacks in this funny place.
Each wave carried giggles like whispers afloat,
A comical voyage, the tales they wrote.

Faint Hues of Distant Horizons

As the sun dipped low, it painted the sea,
A fish wore shades, 'Look at me, look at me!'
Starfish lounged idle, sipping on brine,
While a crab tried to surf but fell out of line.

The sea breeze chuckled, 'What a grand view!'
A seagull squawked, 'Let's party, woo-hoo!'
Bubbles burst forth from a clam in delight,
As waves sloshed around under moon's mellow light.

A soft giggle echoed from the deep blue,
The horizon painted with each joke anew.
In the laughter of sea life, stories align,
Creating a canvas where humor does shine.

The Last Breath of a Dying Wave

A wave once full of zest,
Now gasps its final fling,
It trips on tiny rocks,
And sighs, 'Oh, I can't swim!'

Its friends just stand and cheer,
While seagulls steal its snack,
The ocean laughs along,
As foamy memories crack.

The shore rolls back its eyes,
As laughs merge with the tide,
The wave, in all its pride,
Was just a water ride.

But as the sun sets low,
It leaves a sparkle bright,
A silly, swaying bow,
To bid the day goodnight.

Melodies from the Abyss

Beneath the waves so deep,
Where fish compose a tune,
A crusty crab does clap,
To melodies in June.

The octopus conducts,
With arms a-waving wide,
Each note a bubble burst,
As seaweed starts to glide.

The dolphins join the fun,
With flips and silly grins,
A symphony of laughs,
Where silence never wins.

The anchor's dropped for fun,
While barnacles do hum,
In underwater world,
Silly rhythms become.

In Search of the Gentle Swell

On a surfboard I set sail,
Hunting for the mellow wave,
But met a pile of eels,
Who giggled and did rave.

A gentle swell I'd dreamt,
Instead met bouncing fish,
They teased me with their fins,
And made my balance swish.

I paddled here and there,
Each splash a joyful jest,
The ocean cranked up laughs,
Forget my surfing quest!

At sunset, waves retreat,
With chuckles in the air,
I found a silly swell,
That tickled with a flare.

Lanterns Adrift on the Water's Edge

Little lanterns float free,
Like jellybeans on a spree,
A dance with ripples near,
As giggles fill the sea.

They bob, they weave, they play,
With shadows chasing light,
All glitter and delight,
In this comical flight.

The moon hangs round and sweet,
The tide hums jokes untold,
As lanterns waltz and twist,
In laughter small and bold.

Tomorrow brings the tide,
These lanterns fade away,
But in the hearts they leave,
Fun memories at bay.

The Gaze of Silent Seas

The waves are winking, what a sight,
They gossip softly, day and night.
Seagulls swoop down, steal my fries,
While fish wear sunglasses, oh what a guise!

The shells tell tales of ocean lore,
Of mermaids dancing on the shore.
Crabs tap dance with a nimble sway,
While turtles laugh at their slower way.

With a splash, the dolphins shine,
They play tag with the octopus, feeling fine.
But beware the whale with a sneeze so loud,
It sends all fish to swim away proud!

So when the tide rolls in quite high,
I'll join the fish and wave them bye.
For in this sea of jokes and glee,
Life swims along with such esprit!

Forgotten Odes to High Tides

The moon exclaims, 'What a grand joke!',
As tides make water dance and poke.
Jellyfish float like balloons on strings,
While starfish debate the meaning of swings.

The seaweed sways, a wiggle parade,
A funky display, they'd never trade.
Old boats giggle, bobbing along,
As barnacles grumble a crusty song.

The tide pool hosts a clam's fine feast,
Where all the weird critters come at least.
They argue over snacks, such a sight,
Who knew the flatfish could throw a bite?

With every wave, a new laugh found,
The ocean's humor, a silly sound.
So here we sit, beneath the moon's glow,
In the kooky tidal show, we flow!

Songs of the Silted Bottom

Down where the silt brings laughter low,
The flounder jokes, 'Look at my glow!'
Mud bubbles giggle, rise and pop,
While the eel's dance would make you stop!

Shrimp throw parties in the murky depths,
With treasure chests full of silly preps.
They shake it up like they're on the floor,
Who knew the sea had a dance to score?

Clams play cards, their pearls on the line,
Each bluff and giggle, oh so divine!
The snail sings slow, a ballad of fun,
While the turtle top hat spins in the sun.

As bubbles rise up, like joy in the air,
This silted theatre, beyond compare.
From bottom to top, the laughs tenfold,
In the world beneath, pure fun to unfold!

Mysteries Engulfed by the Depths

What hides in the depths? A fish in a hat!
A race with a squid, oh, imagine that!
Every shadow a riddle, every wave a jest,
The depth's a comedian, dressed in its best.

The octopus juggles with style and flair,
While the grouper just grins, oblivious to care.
Sea cucumbers groove to the beat of the tide,
Shyly they shuffle, their funky pride.

The anglerfish shines like a disco ball,
Inviting all friends for a deep ocean call.
With bubbles exchanged and laughter galore,
Who knew the abyss held such festive decor?

As currents glimmer with fun and delight,
Each twist and turn brings joy to the night.
In the depths of the sea, where mystery brews,
You'll find all the laughs, just dive for the cues!

Odyssey of the Silent Waters

In the quiet depths, fish wear hats,
Swimming in circles like acrobatic cats.
They gossip of sailors who forgot their lines,
Drawing up maps of spaghetti designs.

The bubbles rise up, they giggle and pop,
Talking of turnips that dance and hop.
With laughter so loud, the seaweed sways,
As mermaids tell jokes about their long days.

A clam with a mustache gives wise advice,
While starfish debate the best way to slice.
The tides play along, in a rhythm so bright,
Creating a spectacle, a watery sight.

But beware of the crab that steals the show,
He moonwalks away with a dramatic flow.
In the realm of silence, a party unfolds,
With jokes from the depths that the ocean holds.

The Weave of Wistful Waves

Waves weave together like a patchwork quilt,
Making up tales of mischief and guilt.
A dolphin narrates of a lost bubble's flight,
That vanished too soon in the dead of night.

With a splash and a flip, they jest and play,
Chasing fish friends who slip away.
Starfish applaud with their arms outstretched,
As the seafoam giggles and quietly fetched.

There's a clam that can't stop telling tall tales,
Of treasure-filled ships held captive by snails.
Each tale gets louder as the waves fight back,
While squids pull pranks with their ink-sopping hack.

Thus spun in the laughter of waves on a spree,
Where silliness reigns and the fish drink their tea.
In such a grand fabric, the ocean's delight,
Is stitched with the threads of a whimsical night.

Dances of the Dying Light

As sunhands reach down for the ocean's birth,
Fish gather to celebrate their time on Earth.
They twirl and they dive in a glimmering show,
Where jellyfish jiggle with plenty of glow.

A crab with some flair leads the dance parade,
Waving his pincers like a star on stage.
The seagulls are roped into singing along,
While the starfish tap-dance to a watery song.

In shadows that flicker, the fun never stops,
As octopuses juggle and sea turtle flops.
The evening's enchantment makes laughter take flight,
Beneath all the colors of fading daylight.

And as tides recede, the echoes remain,
Of jokes from the brine that will linger like rain.
So let laughter stretch through this oceanic night,
In the dances of beings who bask in the light.

In the Wake of the Gull's Cry

In the wake of the gull, tales fly high and wide,
A fish spreads the news of a surfboard ride.
He brags of his style on a wave so grand,
While a crab behaves like an impertinent band.

Around comes a pelican, chasing a dream,
Balancing snacks on his beak - what a scheme!
A shrimp starts a rumor of treasures untold,
Hidden beneath layers of stories of old.

The dolphin will flip with a flourish so bright,
Adding to antics that thrill through the night.
Each wave carries laughter on its frothy crest,
With the rhythm of sea life that never will rest.

So heed the gull's call as he squawks on the wind,
For every lost tide has a story to spin.
Laugh with the waves, let your heart intertwine,
In this playful ballet, the ocean's design.

Sunken Echoes in Twilight

A fish once wore a little hat,
Said, "Why not join me, dear old cat?"
The waves just chuckled, dripped with glee,
While crabs danced under the old sea tree.

A lobster tried to sing a tune,
Forgot his words and howled at the moon.
The seaweed swayed, a shimm'ring sight,
At twilight's glance, it all felt right.

A seagull squawked, flew upside down,
Wearing a crown, like the king of town.
But landed soft, on a jelly's back,
And thought, "This is not what I'd unpack."

So let's toast to the waves and their jest,
In twilight's arms, we surely are blessed.
With silly smiles and barnacle friends,
The laughter of the ocean never ends!

The Lament of Ebbing Currents

Oh, the tide pulled back in a huff,
Said, "These shells are getting too tough!"
An octopus, with her eight arms wide,
Tried to juggle fish, but the fish just cried.

A crab with a cane stumbled near,
Yelled, "I swear this sand used to be clear!"
He marched on by, so comically bent,
While shrimp debated where the good food went.

A dolphin laughed, leapt out of sight,
"Soon I'll be dancing at the disco tonight!"
But slipped on seaweed, tumbled and rolled,
Left the tides in stitches, truth be told.

What funny tales the currents weave,
Of sunken dreams and things we believe.
For in these moments, light-hearted chants,
Bring joy amidst the ocean's rants!

Shattered Silhouettes on the Horizon

On the horizon, a fish took flight,
With a sparkly cape, oh what a sight!
He made a splash, like a sea-sick star,
"Maybe I'll dive, or maybe just par!"

A turtle in sunglasses found his groove,
Started to dance, but forgot his move.
He moonwalked right into a passing wave,
Shouted, "I'm trendy, just a bit brave!"

A whale sent postcards from distant shores,
Saying, "Come visit, there's so much more!"
But the seals wrote back with a big wet slap,
"Only if you promise no devious trap!"

Yet laughter echoed through salty air,
In shattered shapes, with a whimsical flair.
For even in jest, the ocean aligns,
With funny fables where the sunlight shines!

Unraveled Threads of Blue

Beneath the waves, a sock was lost,
Cried a fish, "Oh, what's the cost?"
It swam in circles, looking quite grand,
In search of a mate, just like planned.

A clam chimed in with pearls of lore,
"Why not fashion a sock couture store?"
With laughter erupting like bubbles explode,
They crafted outfits on a sandy road.

A sea cucumber in a glittery dress,
Twirled about, calling for press.
"Oh, darling seahorse, do look at me!"
While the stingrays giggled with glee.

In tangled threads of silliness, bright,
We dance with the clans 'neath the soft moonlight.
For in the ocean's fun-filled depths,
The laughter of life takes many steps!

The Forgotten Port

In a harbor where boats forgot to float,
Seagulls squawked like they were on some note.
Fish danced clueless in a wobbly way,
Chasing dreams of becoming sushi someday.

Old docks creaked with a ghostly cheer,
While the lighthouse giggled, 'I can't see clear!'
The captain swore he'd find treasure today,
But all he found was his last hat's display.

Barrels rolled, a comical chase,
Undersea critters stuck in a race.
Crabs in tuxedos strutted about,
Waving claws as if yelling, "Check us out!"

So here's to the port that's lost in the laughs,
Where fish tell jokes and seafarers are chaffs.
A patch of joy in the salty breeze,
Where goofy antics come with ease.

Tearful Lullabies of the Maritime

The ocean hums a tune, oh so strange,
With crabs composing while going through change.
Tears from a mermaid make bubbles rise high,
As dolphins gossip while swimming nearby.

An octopus croons with a tentacled grace,
Serenading the waves like it's a race.
With every note, the sea starts to sway,
And barnacles clap like it's a Broadway play.

Stars twinkle and wink at the seashore crowd,
As seaweed dances, being artsy and loud.
Each splash is a giggle, each wave a cheer,
The maritime laughs, for all is sincere.

So drift away on these lullabies bold,
Where fish tell tales of giggles untold.
In tears, there's laughter, in waves, a bond,
In this watery realm, we all respond.

Residue of the Wandering Ocean

On shores where the lost sandals seem to roam,
The ocean sighs, 'You can always come home.'
Buried treasures of sunken deep flip,
Cans of soda and a half-eaten chip.

A jellyfish floats, like a soft, squishy blob,
While crabs negotiate between a snack and a job.
With every tide, new wonders arrive,
Like messages in bottles trying to thrive.

Seashells giggle in a tiny debate,
Who's the best singer, oh isn't it great?
As starfish applaud with their five-pointed hands,
Marine musicians form silly, strange bands.

So wander these shores where the goofballs stray,
With each wave that comes, let fun lead the way.
In the residue left, joy's always the theme,
In the wandering ocean, life's just a dream.

When the Moon Weeps on Water

The moon takes a dip in the shimmering sea,
Making waves of giggles with splashes of glee.
As stars join in, they start to conga,
While fish in tuxes do the cha-cha with drama.

Lunar tears spark joy, a sight to behold,
Creating puddles of silver and gold.
Mermaids toss their hair, like ribbons on air,
Dancing in circles, without a care.

Plankton bloom like tiny disco balls bright,
Every flicker a wink in the wake of the night.
The seaweed sways in a groovy delight,
As the tides tell tales, of laughter and plight.

When the moon sheds a tear, let it fall with mirth,
For laughter and joy, it's always of worth.
In this watery waltz, we float and we glide,
Under moonlit skies, with laughter our guide.

Streams of Forgotten Resilience

Bobbing ducks with quacked finesse,
Made their way through foam and mess.
In puddles deep, they took their stand,
With breadcrumbs tossed from hungry hand.

Amidst the splash, a fish gave chase,
While turtles tripped in their own race.
They laughed aloud at silly sights,
A water ballet on sunny nights.

Each ripple whispered tales of cheer,
Adventures brewed when skies were clear.
With friends so quirky, spirits soared,
In liquid dreams, their hearts adored.

A frog in tux, a toad with flair,
Party hats flying through the air.
In glee, they danced, a lively throng,
In streams of joy, they all belong.

The Solitude of Deserted Boats

A boat sat lonely in the sun,
With half a sail, it weighed a ton.
It dreamed of journeys to the shore,
But naps were better—who needs more?

A seagull perched atop its mast,
Told tales of fish that swam quite fast.
The boat would chuckle, 'I'm a champ,
They can't catch me, I'm just a lamp!'

With weeds and rust, it wore its pride,
Waved goodbye to the rolling tide.
It thought of races that were missed,
But naps in sun? It couldn't resist!

Once sleek and grand, now quite absurd,
It heard the waves whispering word.
In solitude, it found its groove,
A silly boat that couldn't move.

Celestial Ciphers of the Waves

Stars above on waves do dance,
They giggle softly, take a chance.
One wave whispered, 'Look at me!
I'm Shakespeare's ghost—come write with glee!'

The tide replied with clapping hands,
'We're poets too, with million strands!'
A fish leapt up to play a role,
'Just call me Bard of the fishy shoal!'

Moonbeams twinkled, casting light,
On cosmic riddles, bold and bright.
'Shall we write sonnets?' one did ask,
A jellyfish donned a glowing mask.

The oceans laughed, a symphony,
In currents swirling ecstasy.
Under a dome of cosmic rhyme,
They penned their verses, lost in time.

Waters that Whisper Secrets

Beneath the waves, a tattle-tale,
The fishy gossip set to sail.
Shells clacked softly, sharing news,
Of octopuses wearing shoes!

Seaweed danced, a curtain call,
As crabs went swaggering down the hall.
Their claws declared, 'We rule this place,
With style and grace, we set the pace!'

A dolphin chuckled, making waves,
'What fun we're having, oh how it braves!'
They flipped and flopped, with joy so sweet,
While clam shells grooved to the cheeky beat.

Each splash a secret, bright and rare,
With laughter echoing through the air.
In waters deep, where friends convene,
They share their stories, wild and keen.

Driftwood Dreams and Ocean Echoes

A log floats by with a hat on top,
I laugh so hard, I might just drop.
Seagulls squawk like they own the place,
While fishy puns swim through the space.

The ocean's mirror tells tall tales,
Of mermaids in flip-flops and fish with sails.
Crabs dance the cha-cha on sandy shores,
Telling jokes that ignite hearty roars.

Each wave whispers secrets, oh what a sight,
Of octopuses moonwalking, such a delight.
Shells gossip about the snails' speed race,
And dolphins dive in with a grin on their face.

On this beach, laughter fills the air,
Jellyfish juggling without a care.
As driftwood dreams drift lazily near,
The ocean's humor is perfectly clear.

Sentinels of the Forgotten Bay

Old boats rusting, guarding the shore,
Whispering tales of the times before.
Fish try to listen but just swim by,
While turtles join in, oh my, oh my!

A lighthouse stands tall with a wobbly beam,
Claiming it's crafting a grand fishing dream.
Seagulls put on shades and strike a pose,
While crabs take selfies, striking outrageous flows.

The bay's serenade is a humorous tune,
With laughter that dances under the moon.
As waves tickle toes in a playful splat,
We giggle at dolphins who wear a top hat.

Sentinels watch with a chuckle and grin,
As barnacles join in, swaying with sin.
Here in this bay, the forgotten can't hide,
For fun is their legend, and oh what a ride!

Cries from the Whispering Reefs

Coral castles built with such care,
But seaweed grouches, claiming it's unfair.
Starfish debate who's the best at hiding,
While clownfish roll in giggles, confiding.

Whales sing ballads to a curious crowd,
Their harmonies are silly, but they sing loud.
Anemones sway with wiggly grace,
While flatfish lay low, trying to win the race.

The whispers echo, full of jest,
As shrimp crack jokes, they're quite the best.
With every splash, we share a laugh,
In the laughter of reefs, we find our path.

So next time you wander through fishes' abode,
Remember the giggles along the road.
For life under waves is a comical spree,
In the cries of the reefs, wild and free!

Time's Tidal Embrace

The clock runs backwards on the sandy beach,
As sea turtles ponder, oh what a reach!
With shells as their currency, they trade a laugh,
While crabs plan a party and write a giraffe.

The tides waltz together, a charming dance,
While jellyfish giggle, caught in a trance.
Sand dollars gather in a secret club,
Discussing the latest shells they could rub.

In the cool ocean breeze, time takes a break,
As starfish knit scarves for the waves' shaky wake.
Seashells rattle with joy, like tiny chimes,
While fishes throw puns, spinning delightful rhymes.

So hold on tight to the laughable tide,
For each splash is a moment, a joyful ride.
In time's tidal embrace, let glee fill your heart,
For life is a journey, a whimsical art!

Essence of Sailing Moments

The boat just tipped, oh what a sight,
Fish in the air, they took flight!
Captain's hat flew off in a spin,
It seems the gulls know how to win.

Sailing snacks scattered, a big ol' mess,
Sardines escaping, what a distress!
It's a buffet now for the seagull crowd,
As we wave at them, feeling quite proud!

A wave crashed in, wetting my feet,
I look like a penguin, such a treat!
The sun smiles down with a wink and a grin,
Life's just too funny when chaos kicks in!

So if you see a sailor in glee,
Just know it's a dance with the sea!
Laughter is floating, along with the tide,
In this wacky boat, let's enjoy the ride!

When Waters Remember

The ocean remembers, or so they say,
Each wave a giggle, in its own way.
A jellyfish dances, doing its jig,
While a clam opts for a dance, oh so big!

As the tide rolls in, we start to chuckle,
Crabs in tuxedos, giving a shuffle.
Splashing and laughing, a whirlpool of fun,
Who knew the sea could be such a pun?

Old barnacles tell tales, all covered in green,
"Watch out for dolphins, they're quite the scene!"
A treasure chest grins with every new wave,
"Dig me up, sailors, I promise you a rave!"

The waters may whisper, but they're full of cheer,
With jokes from the depths that we all want to hear.
So sail on, dear friend, with laughter your guide,
For beneath every surface, good times often hide!

The Weight of Wandering Currents

Oh, the currents are heavy with tales anew,
Like a gossiping fish, with a point of view.
After getting lost, I ask the waves why,
They chuckle and bubble, "Just give it a try!"

We float on a floatie, it's quite out of style,
As seaweed tickles; we laugh all the while.
A pirate ship sails by, with a parrot that squawks,
"Is this the right way, or just a few blocks?"

The weight of the journey is nothing but fun,
Especially when every fish wants to run!
The currents may wander, but I'll never fret,
For wisdom comes hard, and laughter's the bet!

So here's to the waves and the silly old tides,
With twists and with turns, let's enjoy the rides.
No maps on this trip, just giggles and glee,
In the ocean of life, we're forever free!

Shattered Reflections in the Tides

A broken mirror shines, with a wink and a laugh,
It shows a crab dancing, a true photograph.
The waves giggle back, with a splash and a roll,
As the moon plays peek-a-boo, like a friendly soul.

Reflections can tease, they twist and they dart,
I see a mermaid with a bubblegum heart!
She blows a bubble, it pops in the air,
Leaving me chuckling, with salty hair!

Every ripple distorts, like a funhouse of glee,
The water's a magician, oh what a spree!
Fish in a top hat, fish in a tie,
Waving hello while passing me by.

So let's sail this circus of splashes and beams,
With laughter and whimsy, we'll follow our dreams.
Shattered reflections, who cares about flaws?
In this carnival tide, we embrace the applause!

Memories Carried by the Wind

A squirrel once danced on a tree,
Swapping nuts for a cup of sweet tea.
He donned a tiny top hat and bow,
Then vanished into the breeze with a show.

A crab in a tux walked the shore,
Claiming the seashells were his decor.
He sold them on eBay with a twist,
Bids soared high, could you even resist?

The gulls held a meeting, quite absurd,
Debating the flavor of words unheard.
"Fish and chips!" one cried, "Let's seize the day!"
They flew off while the sun had its say.

A jellyfish donned shades, looking fine,
Swayed to surf music, sipping on brine.
He threw a party beneath the moon's glow,
But forgot how to dance—what a wild show!

Lullabies of Ocean Depths

The sea turtles sang a bedtime tune,
Humming sweet waves under a silver moon.
The clownfish giggled, their voices a whirl,
As seahorses twirled with a swish and a twirl.

A whale made a wish on a starfish's tail,
Promised it'd sail without leaving a trail.
The octopus inked a heartfelt note,
But it turned into art—he can't stay afloat!

A dolphin ached to dive deep for a snack,
But some floating kelp caused a big boating flack.
He slipped on a sea cucumber's crest,
And neighbored a crab who just wouldn't rest.

The conch shell trumpeted dreams of the tide,
While guppies in bow ties swam side by side.
They formed a parade, with bubbles galore,
Who knew the deep was such a fun store?

The Last Call of Wandering Souls

The ghost of a fish swam in dismay,
Searching for snacks but lost every day.
His friends all moved on to deep, dark abysses,
While he chased the bubbles—a tale full of misses.

Up came a mermaid, brushing her hair,
"Hey, Mr. Fish, don't you have flair?"
She flung him a seashell, which glimmered bright,
But he thought it was dinner and launched a bite.

A turtle played poker, to everyone's shock,
With crabby opponents on the old dock.
Chips made of seaweed and juice from a clam,
All bets were off when a rogue wave went 'bam!'

The seagulls tooted their horns, a parade,
While lost little shells roamed, unafraid.
They laughed with the sun as it bid them goodbye,
In this silly ballet beneath the blue sky.

Beneath the Veil of Aqua Dreams

A starfish dreamt he could run a café,
Serving plankton lattes on a sunny day.
His menu was weird, all seaweed and spice,
But the customers left due to lack of advice.

The squid took up knitting, what a sight to behold,
Crafting warm blankets from yarn spun of gold.
But tangled in strands, he slipped with a squish,
Decided to join the local fish dish.

A clam tried to sing, in a voice like a bell,
But only produced a soft, shy shell swell.
The sea urchins joined in, off-key and proud,
Creating a concert that drew quite a crowd.

A blowfish once claimed he could float without fear,
But puffed up too big and got stuck in a pier.
The crabs threw a party, singing and cheer,
For even in trouble, they'd always stay near!

Between the Tides of Dreams

In the sandbox, castles rise,
Yet, here comes a wave in disguise.
The seagulls laugh, oh what a sight,
As my dreams get swept out of sight.

Every bucket's filled with sand,
But it slips right through my hand.
Crabs are dancing, having fun,
While I chase them, trying to run.

The ocean whispers, 'Try again,'
But I just want to train my pen.
Fish are giggling, splashes fly,
As I splash back, thinking, 'Oh my!'

Among these tides, I take my stand,
With jellybeans in the soft sand.
But seaweed whispers, 'Not today,'
So I just eat my dreams, hooray!

The Remnants of Ocean's Desires

A lonely sock upon the shore,
Whispers tales of love and more.
Did it lose a mate to the sea?
Or was it swimming wild and free?

Mussels dream of fancy foes,
While octopuses put on shows.
And crabs perform a silly dance,
As fish all giggle, 'Take a chance!'

A treasure chest, half-buried, waits,
Filled with socks and paper plates.
The waves they crash, yet they all laugh,
'You'll never find your other half!'

Snails on surfboards catch the breeze,
While dolphins play, just doing ease.
Their laughter rolls on every wave,
In this ocean, jesters brave!

Uncharted Veils of the Current

Bubbles float like secrets gone,
Caught in currents, singing songs.
A fish named Fred, with quite the style,
Wears a hat, but not for a while.

The pirate ship, oh what a sight,
Is really just a sail at night.
Mermaids giggle, play their tunes,
With starfish dancing to the moons.

In this stream of whirling dreams,
Everything's bursting at the seams.
Seashells whisper tales so bright,
Of crabs who dance with all their might.

With sea foam laughter all around,
Even the stones jump off the ground.
From under waves, with winks and spins,
The ocean knows just how to win!

Memories that Fade Like the Setting Sun

A bucket list, or was it sand?
The sun sets down, a golden brand.
Flip-flops squeak, oh what a sound,
As twilight dances all around.

Surfboards lie in a tangled heap,
While sunburns blush, and seagulls leap.
Old sunglasses, cracked and worn,
Watch as another day is born.

Every wave, an echo here,
Of laughter lost, yet still so near.
Tales of crabs that dared to roam,
Now tucked away, they call this home.

As night arrives, the shadows play,
But what were plans, well, who can say?
With salty dreams, we laugh and run,
Chasing memories just as they shun.

Lost Horizons of the Sea

A pirate's hat flies, oh what a sight,
Chasing seagulls that take flight.
A fish did wink, with a sly old grin,
Claiming to be a master of sin.

Sunken treasures, lost in the sand,
Mermaid's hair, a tangled strand.
Shrunken crabs dance under the moon,
Whispering jokes to the fishy tune.

A ship sails past made of jelly beans,
Yelling, "Who's got the best of schemes?"
The octopus juggles, and turtles cheer,
Their laughter echoes for all to hear.

So raise a toast to the waves so bright,
Where humor flows in the salty night.
For in the depths of the ocean's gleam,
A silly dance is the sailor's dream.

The Lure of the Distant Horizon

Oh, the horizon calls with a giggle and tease,
Catching starfish that tickle the knees.
A crab with a monocle, sipping fine wine,
Keeps asking if we'll share the divine.

Seashells would chatter while flapping their tails,
Boasting of dolphins with magical scales.
A penguin dressed dapper shimmies by night,
Claiming to know how to dance in flight.

Every wave giggles, every foam's a jest,
With fish telling tales of the ocean's best.
A treasure chest full of candy awaits,
Game on, my friends; there's no need for mates.

So sail on to the edge where the sky does blend,
Where laughter and waves are the perfect blend.
The distant horizon's a whimsical show,
Making merry where the wild winds blow.

Haunting Lullabies of the Shore

At twilight, the gulls sing a song of delight,
A friendly ghost strums a tune at night.
The seashells hum, echo whispers of lore,
While sandcastles sway on the sandy floor.

A crab in a tuxedo tiptoes through sand,
During the soirée, he took a bold stand.
With a wink and a bow, he's truly a sight,
Inviting jellyfish to dance in the light.

Stars twinkle down like confetti from space,
Ghostly fish join in the merry race.
Glowworms light the path with winks so bright,
While shadows of waves cast a comical fright.

In haunted waters where giggles ring true,
The lullabies lull all the critters anew.
So rest your head, let your worries release,
For the shore holds a laughter that never will cease.

Fables of the Ocean's Edge

Once upon a time, a whale brewed tea,
With crumpets afloat, what a sight to see!
A fish in a bowtie recited a rhyme,
While waves danced along to the rhythm of time.

An octopus known for its quirky attire,
Told tales of the sea like a true sea squire.
The starfish clapped, with their limbs all aglow,
Joining in laughter with a glittery show.

Sea turtles erupted in fits of delight,
Competing in races till the fall of night.
Their shells were adorned with stickers galore,
Every splash echoed laughter on the shore.

So gather ye near by the light of the moon,
Where humor and fables in unison swoon.
At the ocean's edge, let your laughter ring free,
For every tale spun holds a sprinkle of glee.

Secrets of the Silent Sea

Bubbles rise with a giggly cheer,
A fish tells tales, but who can hear?
The crab wears sunglasses, oh what flair,
In this underwater, wacky affair.

Seashells gossip, whisper in glee,
The dolphin dances, wild and free.
A starfish tries its best to groove,
While the seaweed shakes, it's got the move!

Coral chuckles, what a snarky sight,
The octopus juggles with all its might.
Fish in bow ties swim with style,
Making waves, they pause and smile.

So if you're ever by the briny blue,
Just watch the antics, there's more than a few.
Laugh with the tides, let your worries flee,
Beneath the surface, it's a comedy spree!

Reflections on a Starlit Lagoon

In moonlit waters where frogs don capes,
They hold a concert, full of shapes.
A fish in a tux, what a sight to see,
Crickets dance, oh, so carefree!

Stars twinkle down like winking sparks,
As turtles play chess with forgotten marks.
The night owl hoots, "It's time to jest!"
While the drunk firefly claims he's the best.

The lilies giggle, they can't contain,
As beetles race on a splashy train.
True friendships formed in the twilight bloom,
In this starlit dance, there's always room!

So join the party, embrace the delight,
Where laughter rides on the cool night.
In nature's theater, enjoy the show,
Under skies where the funny winds blow!

The Gentle Caress of Time

Tick-tock said the clam with a shell most wise,
While the seagull winks with mischievous eyes.
A jellyfish sways, lost in its thought,
In a dance that time surely forgot.

Seashells tickle those feet that roam,
As a pufferfish ponders its ocean home.
With starry dreams, the barnacle waits,
For it knows, great adventure awaits!

A crab with a clock's face looks divine,
He beeps and bops, stealing the line.
"Time's not a tyrant," he shouts with glee,
"Let's jump into the waves, come swim with me!"

So laugh with the currents as seconds bend,
With each gentle caress, my friend, just pretend.
In the waves of time, there's fun in the flow,
Beneath the surface, let the giggles grow!

Sighs from the Ocean Floor

Anemones sigh with soft-spoken dreams,
While a turtle snickers at the funniest schemes.
The clams gossip, pearls spinning their tales,
While the sea cucumbers hold their scales.

Bubbles rise up with each silly thought,
As the anglerfish parties, with lights so fraught.
A parrotfish giggles, "Look at my teeth!"
While the octopus colors, oh what a wreath!

The sea stars are crafting their own TV show,
With soap Opera crabs bringing drama below.
Sharks in tuxedos swim with great grace,
In this deep ocean, life's a funny race!

So delve into laughter, let worries unfurl,
Below the waves, there's a jesting pearl.
With each sigh you hear from oceany lore,
Remember, the fun's waiting on the ocean floor!

Lament of the Wandering Gull

A gull with a hat, quite dapper and spry,
Sipped soda with friends, while the beach went awry.
He tried to catch fish with a wink and a smile,
But they laughed at his antics, swam off with style.

With a squawk and a flail, he danced with delight,
Chasing crabs in the surf on a warm, sunny night.
He dropped all his snacks, much to seagull glee,
As they swooped and they dove, shouting, "Look, it's free!"

His dreams were of sushi, a feast to behold,
Instead ended up with a taco, quite old.
He pondered his fate in a bucket of fries,
Yet no one could see the tears in his eyes.

Now he soars in the wind, with a chuckle so loud,
For a life full of joy has made him quite proud.
So if you see him, tipping his hat,
Join in on the fun, and sit down for a chat.

Phantoms of the Ebbing Tide

The tide whispers secrets of long-lost fun,
Where shadows of youngsters laugh, run, and run.
With plastic shovels, they build castles so grand,
Only to be washed away by the sea's hand.

A crab, with a grin, steals a child's ice cream,
While the sun dips low, in a hazy daydream.
The kids all chase after, shouting in jest,
As the crab makes his stand—oh, he's truly blessed!

Once a mermaid, who fancied a dance,
Thought humans were charming and gave them a chance.
But her foot got stuck in a clam on the shore,
And now she just giggles, wanting to soar.

So if you hear laughter where waves meet the land,
It's phantoms of fun from a long-ago band.
Join them in frolic, let your worries slide,
For the secrets of merriment flow with the tide.

Unseen Journeys of the Nautilus

In a shell like a bus, rides a nautilus crew,
With snacks made of sand, and a view that's askew.
They travel in circles, no map in their hand,
Spinning tales of the ocean, quite festive and grand.

A clam in pajamas claims he's the best,
While sea cucumbers snore through their underwater quest.
They sing silly songs about bubbles and foam,
And dream of the day they'll all find their home.

As seahorses tango, the octopus jives,
The nautilus chuckles, "We're full of surprises!"
With every new wave, a giggle is born,
In the deep azure world where no one feels worn.

So raise your shell-high, to the friends of the sea,
Whose unseen adventures are wild and carefree.
Join in on the fun, embrace the unique,
For the life of the nautilus is truly mystique!

Memories Lost in the Undertow

Once a starfish named Bill had a wish to relive,
The time when he kicked with the wave's festive give.
With memories hazy of kayak and fun,
He lounged on the beach, soaking up the sun.

Every splash from a kid made him wiggle with glee,
But the tide playfully teased, tossed him straight to sea.
He tumbled and swirled in a flurry of play,
Thinking, "I'm headed to school—guess I'll take the day!"

With jellyfish dancing and dolphins that chat,
Bill realized he missed his warm cozy mat.
But oh, what a journey, through laughter and light,
He waved to his friends, all adrift in delight.

So next time you wander by the ocean's embrace,
Remember the joys, and the silly, sweet grace.
For memories may fade like the clouds in the blue,
But the fun of today makes the best of life's view.

www.ingramcontent.com/pod-product-compliance
Lightning Source LLC
Chambersburg PA
CBHW060141230426
43661CB00003B/525